NEW VANGUARD 310

ESSEX-CLASS AIRCRAFT CARRIERS 1945–91

MARK STILLE   ILLUSTRATED BY ADAM TOOBY

OSPREY PUBLISHING
Bloomsbury Publishing Plc
Kemp House, Chawley Park, Cumnor Hill, Oxford OX2 9PH, UK
29 Earlsfort Terrace, Dublin 2, Ireland
1385 Broadway, 5th Floor, New York, NY 10018, USA
E-mail: info@ospreypublishing.com
www.ospreypublishing.com

OSPREY is a trademark of Osprey Publishing Ltd

First published in Great Britain in 2022

A catalog record for this book is available from the British Library.

ISBN: PB 9781472845818; eBook: 9781472845825;
ePDF 9781472845795; XML: 9781472845801

22 23 24 25 26 10 9 8 7 6 5 4 3 2 1

Index by Rob Munro
Typeset by PDQ Digital Media Solutions, Bungay, UK
Printed and bound in India by Replika Press Private Ltd.

Osprey Publishing supports the Woodland Trust, the UK's leading woodland
conservation charity.

To find out more about our authors and books visit
www.ospreypublishing.com. Here you will find extracts, author
interviews, details of forthcoming events and the option to sign up for
our newsletter.

CONTENTS

ESSEX-CLASS AIRCRAFT CARRIERS 1945–91

INTRODUCTION

The Essex class was the most numerous class of fleet carriers ever built. Based on the successful Yorktown class from 1937, design work on what would become *Essex* began in June 1939. The primary design feature was the capability to embark a large air group and operate it efficiently. The final design was an unqualified success – a ship of some 27,100 tons with the ability to carry an air group of up to 100 aircraft, a range of 15,000 nautical miles (nm) at 15 knots, and a top speed of 33 knots. In addition to speed, range, and striking power, the ship was well-protected and carried a heavy battery of antiaircraft guns. Coupled with the productivity of American shipyards, the Essex class led the way to victory in the Pacific. Though several ships were damaged during the war, two severely, none were sunk.

The lead ship, *Essex*, was ordered in 1938. Three more Essex-class ships were ordered as part of the Two Ocean Navy Act of June 1940. After the fall of France, seven more were funded in August 1940. Another two were funded after the Japanese attack on Pearl Harbor. In August 1942 an additional ten ships were funded followed by three more in June 1943. Of these 26 ships, 24 were completed. Seventeen were commissioned before the end of World War II, and 14 arrived in the Pacific in time to see combat. Another six were canceled before their construction began.

Following the end of hostilities, the USN had no need for a huge carrier fleet. Most Essex-class ships were placed in reserve by 1947. Only five ships completed after the war were kept in service. When war broke out on the Korean peninsula in June 1950, only four Essex-class carriers were active. All saw action in the Korean War. The advent of war opened enough funding to return all but two of the Essex-class ships to active duty. During the 1950s the class underwent a series of modernization schemes.

With 22 ships in commission, the Essex class was the USN's backbone throughout the 1950s until the supercarriers began to enter service in the early 1960s. With the supercarriers in service, the Essex class was

Essex-class carriers provided the USN with the striking power necessary to advance across the Pacific in World War II. This is *Essex* at anchor at Majuro Atoll, March 2 1944, with other ships of Task Force 58. This view of *Essex* shows the World War II configuration. With the addition of extra 40mm quad mounts and upgraded electronics, this is how *Essex* appeared at the end of the war. (Naval History and Heritage Command)

relegated to secondary roles, but they still provided a sizeable portion of USN air power during the Vietnam War. A single Essex-class carrier served until 1991 as the USN's training carrier. Four of these ships still exist today as museum ships.

DESIGN AND DEVELOPMENT

Essex-class carrier modernization

The family tree of the Essex class is complex because of the number of ships in the class, their many roles, and the different modernizations given to them. A total of 32 Essex-class ships were authorized to be built. Construction began on 26; work on *Reprisal* and *Iwo Jima* was stopped in 1945. *Reprisal* was some 50 percent complete but work on *Iwo Jima* had just begun. Construction of *Oriskany* was suspended at the end of the war when the ship was 85 percent complete. It was finally completed in 1950 as the template for the Essex-class modernization program.

Of the 23 Essex-class carriers completed during or right after the war, 14 were modernized as part of the SCB 27A or SCB 27C schemes. Eight received SCB 27A upgrades and another six the SCB 27C modernization work. The next phase of modernization was the SCB 125 program. Of the eight SCB 27A ships, seven subsequently received SCB 125 work. All six ships that received the SCB 27C work also received additional modernization under the SCB 125 program. In general, ships that received SCB 27A modernization ended up being designated CVS and most ships that received SCB 27C work were used as attack carriers. Of the ships receiving SCB 125 work and the *Oriskany* that received the unique SCB 125A modernization, most received the CVS designation.

Nine ships were not modernized. *Franklin* and *Bunker Hill* were the two most heavily damaged ships from the war. Both were retired in 1947 and never returned to service. Since both were fully repaired, the reason for not being recommissioned was not due to any enduring battle damage, but because

USN-carrier designations

All USN ships receive a type designation. Designations for carriers have evolved since the first carrier *Langley* was commissioned in 1922. The original designation CV denoted a ship designed to operate fixed-wing aircraft. This was the original designation given to Essex-class carriers. On October 1 1952, all CVs were redesignated CVA – attack aircraft carriers. Not all carriers operated in an attack role; some Essex-class carriers were later designated as antisubmarine warfare support aircraft carriers (CVS) and were dedicated to antisubmarine warfare (ASW). Some Essex-class ships gained a new role to support amphibious operations and were given the designation amphibious platform helicopter (LPH). The longest-serving Essex-class ship, *Lexington*, was dedicated to training duties and was designated as a training carrier (CVT). Before being decommissioned, some Essex-class ships received the designation as auxiliary aircraft transports (AVT), though none operated in this role. In addition to its designation, each carrier was given a sequential hull number. Thus, *Essex* became CV 9.

Most Essex-class ships underwent modernization overseen by the Ship's Characteristic Board (SCB) established in 1945 to coordinate the design and construction of USN ships. The SCB assigned numbers to its projects beginning in 1946.

By 1950, all but four Essex-class ships were in reserve. This view from 1948 of the Puget Sound Navy Yard in Washington shows six carriers in the "Mothball Fleet" including (from the foreground) *Essex*, *Ticonderoga*, *Yorktown*, *Lexington*, *Bunker Hill*, and in the distance, *Bon Homme Richard*. Of these, all but *Bunker Hill* were returned to service. (Naval History and Heritage Command)

their recent reconstruction made them candidates for a major modernization project that never occurred. *Boxer*, *Leyte*, *Antietam*, *Princeton*, *Tarawa*, *Valley Forge*, and *Philippine Sea* were among the last ships completed, and constituted most of the ships left in commission after 1947. They received only minor modernization. Of note, *Antietam* received the USN's first angled deck in 1952.

Essex-class modernization programs

Following World War II, the USN saw a dramatic decrease in funding. There was no prospect of having new carriers funded, so to maintain its carrier force and lead in naval aviation, the USN was forced to rely on an extensive modernization plan for its existing carriers. The end of the war also brought a new era in naval aviation – the introduction of jet aircraft. It was increasingly difficult for Essex-class carriers to operate jet aircraft as they became faster and heavier, so a modernization program was essential if the class was to remain relevant.

The differences between jets and propeller-driven aircraft were dramatic, and they drove the Essex-class modernization program. The first major difference was how jets handled around the ship. The increased weight of jet aircraft and their slow acceleration speed meant that the traditional rolling take-off was no longer possible. This meant that catapults were required for all launches.

Enabling high-speed jet operations

It took the development of steam catapults, angled decks, and a mirror landing system to enable modern jets to fly safely from aircraft carriers. The first jets to operate off USN carriers were straight-wing aircraft with low landing speeds. They were also slow to accelerate so required catapults for launch. When aircraft incorporated swept wings, their air speed increased, making landings on straight-deck carriers increasingly perilous. Angled decks revolutionized naval aviation. The concept was developed by the Royal Navy and refined by the USN. It was a vital development on the path to safely operate high-speed aircraft from carriers. On a straight-deck carrier, an aircraft could either recover safely by engaging one of the arresting wires or hit the crash barrier, which was always rigged to protect any aircraft parked forward. Using an angled deck, the landing aircraft immediately applied full power after hitting the deck to take off again if an arresting wire was not engaged. Thus, the aircraft either landed safely or went around for another try. The USN began to examine the angled-deck concept in 1951 and after promising test trials on land decided to convert *Antietam* with a 10.5° angled deck in 1952. The conversion was successful but was considered experimental, not a modernization.

The final component required to operate high-speed jets was the development of the mirror landing system. This was also first developed by the British. A large mirror was placed at the edge of the angled deck and gyro stabilized to compensate for the ship's movement. When light was projected on the mirror, it produced a beam that the pilot could aim for. A horizontal row of light on either side of the lights gave the pilot a horizontal reference.

Antietam was the first carrier in the world to operate aircraft with an angled deck. Previous tests on a Royal Navy carrier and on *Midway* used an angled deck painted on the flight deck for touch-and-go landings. This view of *Antietam* in January 1953 shows the first true angled deck created by the addition of a port-side sponson with the arresting gear oriented on the angled deck. (Naval History and Heritage Command)

The existing H4 catapults on the Essex class did not possess the power to launch heavier jets. Heavier aircraft and higher landing speeds translated into a requirement for more powerful arresting gear. Other internal requirements to handle jet aircraft included greater storage for aviation gasoline, and later for jet fuel. Larger pumps were required to speed the refueling of jets.

In the early years of the Cold War, nuclear weapons became a paramount factor in US military planning and budgeting. The USN needed to field nuclear weapons to remain competitive against the US Air Force in the budgeting wars during a period of austere funding. One of the immediate answers was to deploy bombers on carriers with the range and payload to strike the Soviet Union. These large aircraft needed more powerful catapults and arresting gear. The atomic bombs carried aboard these aircraft needed heavier weapons elevators and special storage and assembly areas.

There were also wartime lessons that the USN wanted incorporated into any carrier modernization. Among the most important was improved side armor, movement of the elevators from the centerline to the deck-edge, and protected ready rooms for the air crew. The wartime antiaircraft suite had to be improved. The 5in./38 guns were retained, but the 40mm quad mounts were replaced with twin 3in./50 mounts. Several types of missiles were also considered for Essex-class carriers, including antiaircraft missiles for self-defense and long-range cruise missiles and ballistic missiles able to carry nuclear weapons.

Essex-class modernization design work began as early as February 1945. By October 1946, two studies were completed, one featuring an austere modernization for $25 million per ship, and a more complex upgrade costing $33 million. Given budget constraints, only the austere scheme was possible, and only after it was modified to reduce costs. This became known as SCB 27A. *Oriskany*, construction of which was suspended after the war, was used as a prototype for carrier reconstruction. This work was included in the Fiscal Year (FY) 48 program. For the FY 49 program, *Essex* and *Wasp* were taken out of reserve for modernization. To save money, it was planned that the FY 50 program would use ships already in service. *Kearsarge* was decommissioned for this purpose, but the second ship, *Leyte*, could not be withdrawn from service because of the Korean War. That place was taken by *Lake Champlain*. Whatever ships were used, SCB 27A was still expensive. Actual costs varied from the $112 million to finish *Oriskany* to $38 million to modernize ships pulled from active service. To reduce costs, several less expensive modernization schemes were examined. There was also a considerable time commitment for a full SCB 27A modernization – two years in the yard.

Despite the rising costs, modernization was essential to making Essex-class ships viable in the jet age, so the SCB 27A program continued. Originally planned for seven ships, this was increased to nine in May 1950. When the Korean War broke out the following month, funding was no longer a problem. Four SCB 27A modernizations were authorized for FY 51 and four more the next FY. By the time the final two SCB 27A conversions were authorized as part of the FY 53 program, costs had risen to $63 million per ship. A more austere modernization scheme, SCB 27B, was dropped.

This is *Yorktown* after SCB 27A modernization before being deployed to the Western Pacific in September 1953. During modernization, the island was rebuilt, and the flight deck 5in./38 twin mounts were removed. Note the starboard side single 5in./38 mounts and the 3in. twin mounts. The bow is not enclosed but was in the next modernization. Two Mark 37 fire control directors can be seen on the island. Other electronics include the World War II-era SC-5 and SPS-6 air search radars, and the SPS-8A height-finder radar. (Naval History and Heritage Command)

Description of SCB 27A

Nine ships received this modernization between 1948 and 1953: *Essex, Yorktown, Hornet, Randolph, Wasp, Bennington, Kearsarge, Oriskany*, and *Lake Champlain*. The principal aspects of this package were:

- Replacing the Type H-4B catapults with the Type H-8 allowing the launch of aircraft up to 20 tons.
- Installation of blast deflectors behind the catapults.
- Replacing the Mark 4 with Mark 5 arresting gear.
- Enlarging the size of the centerline elevators to 58 x 44ft and increasing their capacity to 40,000lb.
- Increasing the capacity of the deck-edge elevator to 30,000lb.
- Strengthening the flight deck to handle aircraft up to 52,000lb.
- Installation of a mirror landing system.
- Installation of two fireproof bulkheads and improved fire curtains in the hangar deck and a new fire-fighting system.
- Movement of three aircrew ready rooms from under the flight deck to under the hangar deck armor. An escalator was added outside the island to move the pilots from their ready rooms to the flight deck.
- The forward bomb elevator was increased in size and capacity to handle nuclear weapons (this was not fitted to all ships).
- Internal aviation gasoline capacity was increased to 300,000 gallons.
- Removal of the 4in. side armor from the hull.
- The island was reduced in size and a massive pole mounted on top to support the installation of radars without the interference problems evidenced during the ships' wartime configuration.
- Removal of the four twin 5in./38 mounts on the flight deck and addition of sponsons on the starboard side to bring the 5in. battery to eight single 5in./38 guns. All 40mm quadruple mounts were removed and replaced with 14 twin 3in./50 mounts.
- Hull blisters added to increase stability.

Studies begun in 1951 started the momentum for more upgrades beyond the SCB 27A work. This modernization package became known as SCB 27C. The new program added a more powerful catapult, new arresting gear, and a new starboard-edge elevator with a greater lift capacity replacing the previous centerline elevator. All this further increased displacement and reduced the margins of stability. To compensate, new 5ft-wide hull blisters were fitted, but this reduced top speed to 30.6 knots. Reduced stability translated into a reduced ability to handle damage. It was estimated that only two torpedo hits would create a list of 21 degrees.

Hancock was the prototype for the SCB 27C package. Conversion of the next two ships to SCB 27C, *Intrepid* and *Ticonderoga*, was almost delayed by work on the new catapult, but this situation was rectified by the arrival of the new C 11 steam catapult. This system could launch 39,000lb aircraft at 136 knots or a heavier 70,000lb aircraft at 108 knots. The antiaircraft

A

***ESSEX* IN 1951**

Essex was one of the first ships to receive the SCB 27A modernization. As shown in these views, the ship was fitted with a new and larger island and has an electronics suite mainly based on World War II radars. SPS-6B and SC-5 air search radars were placed on the new pole mast with the SX height-finder radar forward of the pole mast. An SG-6 was fitted for surface search. The two Mark 37 directors, used to control the 5in. battery, are also located on the island. The World War II -era 40mm quad mounts have been replaced by 3in./50 mounts; a total of 14 were initially fitted. This includes two mounts on the open bow, which were soon removed.

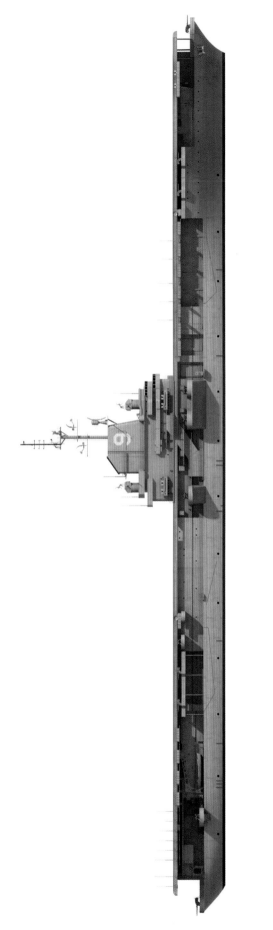

battery of the SCB 27Cs with an angled deck was reduced to eight 5in./38 and only five twin 3in./50 mounts.

The first three SCB 27C conversions had an open bow configuration, but these were later retrofitted with the hurricane bow and an angled deck. The second group of three ships received the hurricane bow and an angled deck as part of their SCB 27C work. An enclosed hurricane bow provided improved seakeeping. During World War II, the edges of several Essex-class ships had been smashed by severe storms. The hurricane bow flared the hull into the forward part of the flight deck. A secondary conning station was fitted in the most forward space directly under the flight deck.

The next step in Essex-class modernization was to get steam catapults on the SCB 27A ships and provide them with the angled deck they needed to operate modern aircraft. This was the SCB 125 conversion, which also included the provision of a hurricane bow and a starboard deck-edge elevator abaft the island in place of the aft centerline elevator. The antiaircraft battery was reduced to seven 5in./38 single mounts (one was removed from the aft starboard sponson) and five twin 3in./50 mounts to compensate for the added weight.

SCB 125 was the largest Essex-class modernization with 13 ships affected. This was rolled out in three different groups. The first was *Lexington*, *Bon Homme Richard*, and *Shangri-La* which received the SCB 125 package during the same yard period they received their SCB 27C work. The second group included *Intrepid*, *Ticonderoga*, and *Hancock*, which received the SCB 125 upgrade

This port beam view of *Randolph* is from July 1 1953 on the day of recommissioning following the SCB 27A modernization. Note the lack of a hurricane bow and a full complement of 5in./38 and 3in./50 mounts. The typical SCB 27A electronics suite of the SPS-12 air search radar, the SPN-6 air traffic control radar, and the SPS-8 height finder is visible. (Naval History and Heritage Command)

between 1955 and 1957. A third group was comprised of seven ships that had earlier received the SCB 27A modernization. These ships did not receive all the previous improvements from SCB 27C. This group included *Essex*, *Yorktown*, *Hornet*, *Randolph*, *Wasp*, *Bennington*, and *Kearsarge*. Work on these ships was completed between 1954 and 1957.

Oriskany, *Shangri-La*, *Hancock*, and *Bon Homme Richard* were the last Essex-class carriers to retain an attack role. The final configuration of the attack carriers included three or four 5in./38 single mounts, the massive SPS-43A air search radar, and an enlarged flight control station on the aft portion of the island.

The SCB 125A program added all the improvements of SCB 125 and some from SCB 27C. It was a conversion unique to *Oriskany*. In addition to the list of SCB 125 modifications, it gave the ship steam catapults, an angled deck, the hurricane bow, and more powerful arresting gear.

Comparison of Essex-class modernization programs

	SCB 27A	SCB 27B	SCB 125	SCB 125A
Ships receiving	*Essex, Yorktown, Hornet, Randolph, Wasp, Bennington, Kearsarge, Oriskany, Lake Champlain*	*Intrepid, Ticonderoga, Lexington, Hancock, Bon Homme Richard, Shangri-La*	*Essex, Yorktown, Intrepid, Hornet, Ticonderoga, Randolph, Lexington, Wasp, Hancock, Bennington, Bon Homme Richard, Kearsarge, Shangri-La*	*Oriskany*
Full load displacement (tons)	40,600	41,944 (43,060 with angled deck)	41,200	44,000
Dimensions in feet (length/beam/draft)	898/152/30	898/167/30	890/196/30	911/157/31
Top speed	31.7 knots	32 knots	32 knots	32 knots
Armament	8 5in./38, 12-14 twin 3in./50	8 5in./38, 12 twin 3in./50 (4 5in./38 after addition of angled deck)	7 5in./38, 5 twin 3in./50	2 5in./38
Elevators	one 34 x 60ft deck edge (46,000lb capacity), two 44 x 58ft centerline (46,000lb capacity)	one 44 x 56ft deck edge (57,000lb capacity), one 34 x 60ft deck edge (46,000lb capacity), one 44 x 58ft centerline (46,000lb capacity)	one 40 x 60ft port side and one starboard side (both 46,000lb capacity), one 44 x 58ft centerline (46,000lb capacity)	as SCB 27A
Catapults	two hydraulic	two steam	two steam	two steam
Crew (ship's company only)	104 officers/2,791 men	131 officers/2,086 men (167 officers and 2,418 men after addition of angled deck)	110 officers/1,980 men	110 officers/1,980 men

ASW carriers

Early in the Cold War, the USN feared the Soviet Navy would deploy a massive number of modern submarines with advanced German technology. The USN planned to counter this threat in a number of ways including the deployment of hunter-killer groups built around a carrier. These groups would react to long-range detections or attacks on convoys, initially with ASW aircraft followed by ASW escorts. Attempts to use World War II escort or light carriers in an ASW role were ineffective. Only Essex-class ships had the space to operate large postwar ASW aircraft in sufficient numbers to accomplish the mission. The problem was that only a few Essex-class ships were available for conversion into ASW platforms, and ASW was (and is) a numbers game. In late 1952, *Valley Forge* was tested in an ASW role and proved very successful. This was primarily because the ship could operate two squadrons of ASW aircraft in all types of wind and weather conditions.

Hunter-killer tactics were built around the aircraft carrier. Four fixed-wing aircraft, four helicopters, and an airborne early warning aircraft were maintained aloft at all times. This required a large air group of ASW aircraft and helicopters. Ideally, eight destroyers were also assigned to the group; four to provide close cover to the carrier and four to prosecute contacts. An Essex-class carrier had enough fuel to keep the destroyers steaming for 12 days and the aircraft flying for eight. Two ships, *Randolph* and *Wasp*, embarked an ASW ship command and control system to oversee operations. Another key ASW modification to the carriers was the addition of a large bow sonar – the SQS-23. With a theoretical active sonar range of 12,000yds, it was used primarily for self-defense. The sonar displayed superior detection capabilities when fitted aboard a carrier (as opposed to a smaller destroyer or frigate) because of its greater depth in the water and the stability of the carrier itself. Exercises revealed the sonar gained solid contact at over 7,000yds and was useful for vectoring in other platforms to engage the target.

All seven of the unmodernized Essex-class ships were redesignated CVS and given ASW roles. Five received the CVS designation in 1953 and two more the following year. The SCB 27A ships also received this designation, beginning with *Wasp* in 1956.

B **_SHANGRI-LA_ IN 1956**

These plates show *Shangri-La* in 1956 following the completion of SCB 27C/125 modernization. The ship has an angled deck and a hurricane bow. Note that there are now two deck-edge elevators and one centerline elevator. The aft elevator is in the folded position. The 5in./38 battery consists of eight mounts, but the 3in./50 battery has been reduced to seven twin mounts. On top of the new island is a pole mast with an SPN-6 precision approach radar and an SPS-6 air search radar. At the base of the mast is a SPS-8A height-finder radar.

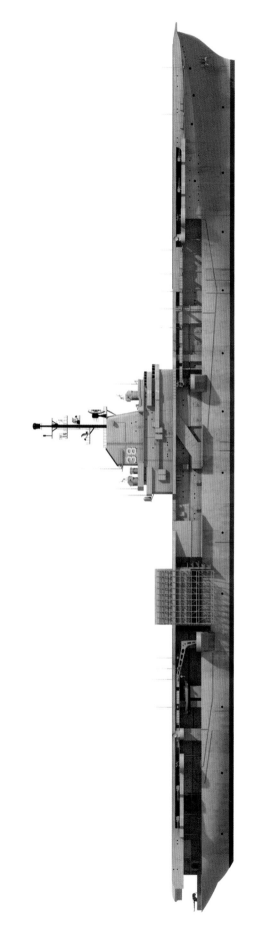
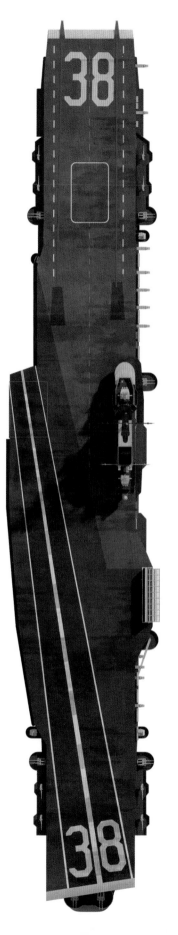

Essex-class ships converted into ASW carriers were the centerpieces of hunter-killer groups formed to conduct intensive ASW operations against Soviet submarines. The most potent ASW weapons in the groups were the S2F Tracker aircraft from the carrier, two of which can be seen ready to launch. Surface escorts were also important to protect the carrier and prosecute contacts. This is *Yorktown* returning from 1967 Western Pacific Deployment. The eclectic group of escorts includes (clockwise from the left of the image) Adams-class guided-missile destroyer *Goldsborough*, Fletcher-class destroyer ASW conversions *Taylor* and *Jenkins*, Dealey-class frigates *Bridget* and *Hooper*, and Bronstein-class frigate *Bronstein*. (Naval History and Heritage Command)

The addition of ASW equipment on CVS ships was done under the SCB 144 program, which was part of the Fleet Rehabilitation and Modernization (FRAM) program. By the 1960s the age of Essex-class ships operating in the ASW role made them prime candidates for the FRAM program, since it was designed to increase the ships' lifespan by a few years. In FY 61, *Randolph* was the first to receive the SCB 144 upgrade in the form of the austere FRAM II modification. Aside from work aimed to enhance habitability, the ships received the SQS-23 and other warfighting improvements. Since this program was much cheaper than building new ships, seven more received FRAM II work – *Essex* and *Kearsarge* in the FY 62 program; *Bennington* in FY 63; *Intrepid*, *Hornet*, *Wasp* in the FY 65 program, and *Yorktown* in FY 66. Only one SCB 27C ship, *Intrepid*, received this work.

The numbers of ASW carriers declined in the 1970s as their effectiveness reduced and the difficulties and cost of maintaining the old ships increased. The Vietnam War consumed funds that might have been used to keep the USN's older ships in service. The final ship converted to an ASW carrier was *Ticonderoga* in 1969. The CVS force was reduced to three ships in the Atlantic Fleet by 1972. *Intrepid* was the last active ASW carrier.

In their final configuration the ASW carriers could be distinguished from the ships equipped with steam catapults by the absence of the two bridle arrester sponsons overhanging the bow. The presence of a bow anchor marked the presence of the large SQS-23 bow sonar. Armament was reduced to four 5in./38 guns with two Mark 56 and two Mark 37 directors.

Amphibious assault carriers

In a war fought under nuclear conditions, the Marine Corps determined that an amphibious assault force would have to be dispersed. However, the requirement to quickly deliver troops to the beachhead remained. The most promising method to accomplish this was by using helicopters. Early tests using World War II escort carriers validated the concept of vertical assault. The need for larger ships to carry more helicopters was addressed when unconverted Essex-class ships were made available for new roles. Two of the original CVSs, *Boxer* and *Princeton*, became assault carriers in 1959 and were redesignated LPH-4 and LPH-5, respectively. *Valley Forge* was shifted to this role in 1961 and redesignated LPH-8.

This was only an interim solution until the Iwo Jima class of helicopter carriers entered service beginning in 1961. Initially an extensive helicopter assault reconstruction was planned, but this would have cost $25 million per ship. Instead, modifications were made to decrease maintenance and operating costs. Accordingly, most of the guns were removed leaving only two of the twin 5in./38 mounts on the flight deck and two single mounts on portside sponsons (*Boxer* retained all four twin 5in./38 mounts and no sponson mounts). The radar suite was reduced, and four of the eight boilers were removed, bringing speed down to 25 knots. A total of 30 helicopters could be embarked and berthing space provided for a Marine battalion landing team.

Essex-class weapons

The Essex class's original design included a heavy defensive antiaircraft battery. This consisted of 12 5in./38 guns (in four twin mounts and four single mounts), eight 40mm quad mounts (later increased to as many as 18 on some ships), and between 46 and 58 single 20mm mounts. The single 20mm mounts were replaced late in the war with twin mounts. Kamikaze attacks late in the war demonstrated the inadequacy of the 40mm and 20mm guns in terms of providing stopping power against onrushing suicide aircraft. In response, the USN developed the 3in./50 twin mount that possessed a high rate of fire and could fire a proximity round. The first of these guns entered service in 1948, replacing the 40mm quad mount.

After serving as an attack and an ASW carrier, *Valley Forge* spent the final almost nine years as an LPH. The carrier is seen here in May 1964 before the first of four Vietnam deployments. There are 14 Marine Corps UH-34 Sea Horse helicopters arrayed on the flight deck. Note all 3in./50 mounts have been removed; only two 5in./38 twin mounts remain around the island and two single 5in./38 single mounts on port-side sponsons. (Naval History and Heritage Command)

Unmodernized Essex-class ships retained their World War II-era antiaircraft battery into the 1950s, but the size of the battery was gradually reduced due to manpower requirements and questions of its effectiveness against modern threats. Modernized ships kept their 5in. single mounts and added the new 3in./50 twin mounts. The prototype for the SCB 27A reconstruction, *Oriskany*, was fitted with eight 5in./38 dual-purpose guns and 14 twin 3in./50 mounts. Subsequent SCB 27A conversions were completed with fewer 3in./50 mounts to reduce top weight. The SCB 27C modernization increased top weight, which forced the 3in./50 battery down to five mounts. Further increases in weight could only be compensated for by the removal of more weapons. Few ships had any of the original 3in./50 mounts by 1960. The 5in./38 battery was also reduced; it possessed little value against modern air attack but was still considered effective against surface craft. Most ships carried only four 5in./38 guns when they left service. The last to retire, *Oriskany*, only carried two. Radar fire control included the Mark 56 director for the 3in./50 and two Mark 37s on the island for the 5in./38 guns.

It is a little-known fact that Essex-class carriers were part of the USN's plan to create a sea-going nuclear deterrent with cruise missiles in the 1950s. The Regulus cruise missile system was placed onboard four Baltimore-class heavy cruisers and five submarines. Four Essex-class carriers were also fitted to launch the Regulus, but the carrier community was not enthusiastic about their use since they already had aircraft to perform the nuclear attack mission and the introduction of Regulus presented problems with handling aircraft on a crowded flight deck. The missile itself was powered by a turbojet that gave it a maximum speed of about 550 knots. It was armed with a single nuclear warhead. The weapon's theoretical range of 500nm was restricted in operational use by the need to be steered by a platform within radio contact.

The first Essex deployment with Regulus occurred in August 1955 when *Hancock* departed for the Western Pacific with four missiles embarked. *Hancock* was the only Pacific Fleet carrier to deploy with Regulus. In the Atlantic Fleet, only *Randolph* made a deployment with Regulus when the ship took three to the Mediterranean. The short-lived era of Regulus onboard carriers came to an end with the introduction of the A-4 Skyhawk attack aircraft in 1956, which was a superior nuclear delivery platform.

ORISKANY IN 1973

Oriskany had the most interesting Cold War career of any Essex-class carrier. Being the last ship of the class to be completed, *Oriskany* became the template for the modernization of 14 other Essex-class ships and was the only Essex-class carrier to receive the SCB 125A modernization. As the most modern ship of the class, serious consideration was made to reactivating the ship in the 1980s when the Reagan Administration was building a 600-ship Navy. After a long career, including service in the Korean War and many combat deployments to Vietnam, *Oriskany* was decommissioned in 1976 and was sunk as an artificial reef in the Gulf of Mexico in 2006.

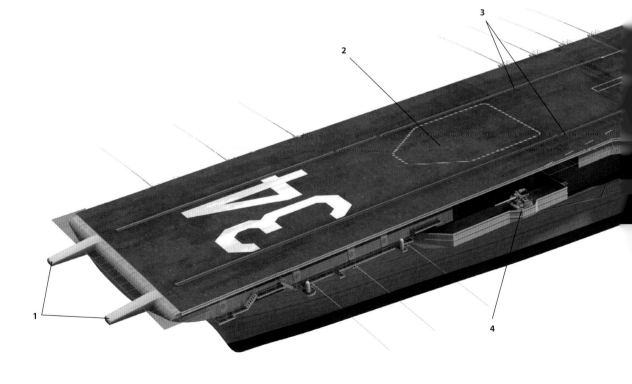

Key

1. Bridle arrestor sponsons
2. Centerline deck elevator
3. C-11 catapults
4. 5in./38 single mount (4)
5. Navigation and flag bridges
6. Mark 37 director with Mark 25 radar (2)
7. SPS-43 air search radar
8. SPS-10 surface search radar
9. SRN-6 TACAN
10. SPN-6 precision approach radar
11. Pole mast
12. SPS-30 height-finder radar
13. Island
14. SPN-35 Air traffic control radar under environmental cover
15. Aircraft crane
16. Starboard-side deck-edge elevator
17. Whip antenna (numerous)
18. Mark 56 director (2)
19. Arresting wires (4)
20. Angled deck
21. Machinery room
22. Boiler room
23. Port-side deck-edge elevator

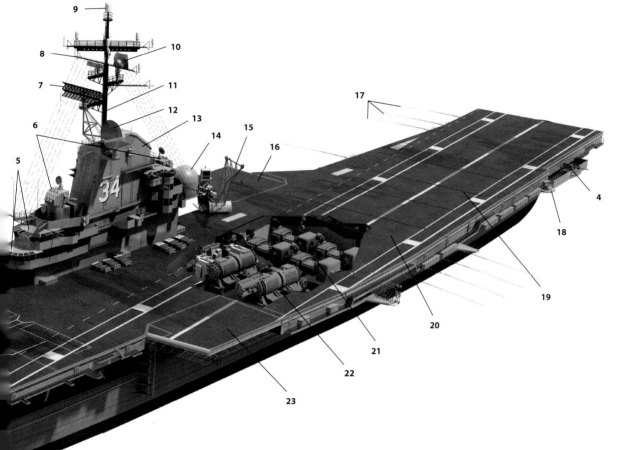

Essex-class radars and sonars

Essex-class radars at the end of World War II included the SK/SK-2 and SC-2 for air search, the SP for height-finding, and the SG for surface search. Unmodernized ships carried some of these radars until they were retired. Given the quick pace of developing new ship-borne radars in the 1940s and 1950s, all Essex carriers received some electronics modernization. Those ships receiving the SCB 27A/C or SCB 125 packages received a new electronics suite.

SCB 27A ships carried most of their electronics on a heavy pole mast on top of the island. This arrangement reduced the mutual interference problem so prevalent with the World War II radar configuration. The first post-war air search radar was the SPS-6A. This was quickly replaced by the SPS-12 in 1953 and then by SPS-29 in 1958. The largest air search radar fitted aboard an Essex-class ship was the SPS-37 with its 42ft-wide antenna. Introduced in 1960, it possessed a detection range of up to 300nm. A handful of ships received the SPS-43, which was an improved SPS-37, but was externally indistinguishable.

Height-finding radars were essential for fighter control. The World War II-era SP was replaced by the SX in the late 1940s. Later height finders consisted of the SPS-8 and finally the SPS-30. The SPS-30 was first delivered in 1962. The SPS-10 became the USN's standard surface search radar when introduced in the early 1950s.

Principal Cold War Essex-class radars		
Radar	Purpose	Maximum range
SPS-6A/B/C	Air search	70–140nm (against large targets)
SPS-8A/B	Height-finding	72nm (actual)
SPS-10	Surface search	8nm (against a periscope-sized target)
SPS-12	Air search	70–90nm (actual)
SPS-29	Air search	270nm (theoretical)
SPS-30	Height-finding	240nm (theoretical)
SPS-37	Air search	233–300nm (actual)

THE ESSEX CLASS IN WAR AND PEACE 1945–1991

The first post-war duties of the Essex-class ships were as part of Operation *Magic Carpet* between October 1945 and May 1946. To bring back troops to the US from overseas, Essex-class carriers were converted into troop transports with the addition of messing and berthing facilities on the hangar deck. A total of 11 ships participated in Operation *Magic Carpet*, operating in both the Pacific and European theaters.

Essex, *Intrepid*, and *Lexington* remained in the Western Pacific after the war to support occupation operations. These veterans were joined by *Antietam* and *Boxer*, which had arrived too late to see combat. At the conclusion of Operation *Magic Carpet*, Essex-class ships with wartime service returned to the US and were placed in reserve by 1947. The last ships to be completed joined *Boxer* and *Antietam* on active service. These included *Leyte*, *Kearsarge*, *Philippine Sea*, *Tarawa*, and *Valley Forge*. Because of severe budget restrictions, by 1950 only four Essex-class ships were still active – *Boxer*, *Leyte*, *Philippine Sea*, and *Valley Forge*.

Essex-class carrier postwar air groups

The USN was quick to enter the jet age in naval aviation. During the 1940s and 1950s, the pace of jet aircraft development resulted in a large number of jet aircraft entering service and being placed on carrier decks. Many of these were found to be unsuitable and were produced in small numbers. Early jets were difficult to operate off carriers because they were underpowered. This made launch and recovery operations a challenge. Since they could not carry heavy loads, early jets operated as fighters with propeller aircraft still being more suitable as fighter bombers. The most common jets of the Korean War era were the McDonnell F2H Banshee and the Grumman F9F Panther, both entering squadron service in 1949.

The Vought F4U Corsair remained in service after World War II and played a major role in Korea. Other USN attack aircraft from World War II were replaced by the Douglas AD Skyraider, which could carry an amazing 8,000lbs of ordnance.

Valley Forge was the first carrier to enter combat in Korea and the ship's air group was typical for the period. It consisted of two squadrons of F9F-2B Panther jets with 30 aircraft, two squadrons of F4U-4B Corsairs with 28 aircraft, a heavy attack squadron with 14 AD4 Skyraiders, and another 14 Corsairs and Skyraiders of different variants for photo-reconnaissance, airborne early warning, and electronic countermeasures work. Total air group strength was 86 aircraft. Later in the war, *Boxer* deployed with three squadrons of the updated Panther (the F9F-5 variant) and one squadron of Skyraiders. The unmodernized carrier was unable to effectively operate three squadrons of jets, so traded one to *Lake Champlain* for a squadron of Corsairs. *Lake Champlain* had been modernized and proved able to operate an air group of two Banshee and one Panther

Hancock during one of the carrier's Western Pacific deployments in July 1957. This view shows the carrier after the SCB 27C/125 modernization. On the flight deck is an array of aircraft from a typical late 1950s air group: seven FJ Fury, ten F2H Banshee, two F7U Cutlass, fifteen AD Skyraider, and three AJ Savage medium bombers. A sign of an SCB 27C/SCB 125 modernization was the two bridle arrestment sponsons projecting from the bow of the ship. This was used to catch the bridle that slung aircraft down the catapult track. If the sponsons weren't present, the bridle would fly into the ocean, which was wasteful. Current carriers do not need the bridle arrestment sponson because the bridle was replaced by a catapult launch bar attached to the aircraft's landing gear. (Naval History and Heritage Command)

squadron, in addition to the usual Skyraider squadron and the assorted special-mission aircraft.

It was immediately apparent that the MiG-15 was a far superior fighter than the USN's first-generation jets so the straight-wing Banshees and Panthers were replaced by heavier and more powerful second-generation swept-wing fighters. These included the F9F-6 Cougar (based on the Panther) and the FJ-2/3 Fury (a naval version of the F-86). Supersonic fighters reached the fleet in the form of the McDonnell F3H-1 Demon, the Douglas F4D Skyray, the Grumman F11F-1 Tiger, and the Vought F7U Cutlass. The last and best fighter to enter service aboard Essex-class carriers was the Vought F8U Crusader. It entered fleet service in 1957 and proved superior to North Vietnamese MiG-17s and MiG-21s.

Strike aircraft also developed rapidly. The Skyraider remained in service into the Vietnam War because of its combination of ruggedness, endurance, and ability to carry a large payload. The USN's desire for a lightweight strike aircraft was filled by the Douglas A4D Skyhawk, which entered service in 1956 and remained on the decks of Essex-class carriers until they left service. Late in the Vietnam War, the A4 was joined by the Vought A7A Corsair II in the light attack role.

Another theme in carrier air group development was the deployment of aircraft to carry nuclear weapons. Early nuclear weapons were large and required large aircraft to carry them. The first nuclear-capable aircraft deployed aboard Essex-class carriers was the North American AJ-1 Savage. This design featured two piston engines and a jet engine in the tail and first embarked on an Essex-class ship in 1951. The largest aircraft to operate from an Essex-class carrier was the twin-engine Douglas A3D Skywarrior. It replaced the Savage in the nuclear attack role. After the size of nuclear weapons was reduced, allowing aircraft as small as the Skyhawk to carry them, the Skywarrior was converted to perform other roles including photo reconnaissance, electronic warfare, and aerial refueling.

For ASW operations, Essex-class carriers initially relied on single-engine Grumman AF Guardians and Skyraiders alongside early helicopters. The introduction of the twin-engine Grumman S2F Tracker represented a major upgrade in carrier-borne ASW. It was large enough to carry radar and magnetic anomaly detection gear to find submarines, and depth charges and torpedoes to attack anything it detected. In the late 1950s, a typical CVS air group consisted of one squadron with 20 S2F Trackers, a squadron of HSS-1 Seabat helicopters, and a detachment of Douglas AD-5W Skyraider airborne early warning (AEW) aircraft. Four F2H Banshees were often embarked to provide limited air defense capabilities. After 1960, the CVS air group evolved into two squadrons of Trackers (each with ten aircraft), a helicopter squadron with either 16 Seabats or the much-improved Sikorsky SH-3 Sea King, and an AEW detachment with three Grumman E-1 Tracers. The small fighter detachment was not embarked between 1960 and 1965. Subsequently, a detachment with A-4 Skyhawk attack aircraft was often added.

ABOVE LEFT
USN airpower was a key factor in the defeat of North Korean forces during their initial onslaught from June to August 1950. Much of this airpower came from TF 77 with its Essex-class carriers. In this view *Valley Forge* and *Leyte* are moored at Sasebo, Japan, circa October–November 1950. *Valley Forge* was the first carrier to respond to the North Korean aggression and was a stalwart throughout the war making a total of four combat deployments. (Naval History and Heritage Command)

ABOVE RIGHT
The most numerous aircraft on the decks of Essex-class carriers for much of the Korean War was the F4U Corsair. This view is of two F4U-5N night fighters flying past *Boxer* on September 4 1951. During operations over Korea, the Corsair was used for ground attack missions using 20mm guns, bombs, and napalm tanks, and unguided (mostly 5in.) rockets. (Naval History and Heritage Command)

Essex-class carriers and the Korean War

Since the three large Midway-class carriers were retained in the Atlantic to deal with the Soviet threat, the Essex class carried the burden of fighting the naval air war in Korea. The USN also deployed light and escort carriers to the region, and the Royal Navy dispatched two light carriers in support of Allied operations, but the Korean War featured the Essex class in a lead role. War broke out on the Korean peninsula on June 25 1950. The only carrier in the region was *Valley Forge*, then located off Hong Kong. Operating from the Yellow Sea, *Valley Forge* aircraft opened the naval air war by striking targets around the North Korean capital of Pyongyang on July 3–4. The flexibility of naval aviation was amply demonstrated when the next series of strikes was conducted off the eastern coast of Korea and included strikes as far north as Wonsan, North Korea. Starting on July 22, the carrier force's (designated Task Force (TF) 77) priority shifted to supporting the hard-pressed defenders in the Pusan Perimeter. The first actual close air support (CAS) missions flown on July 25 were chaotic primarily due to communications problems. Once these were rectified, the fleet carrier provided excellent support to the 8th Army inside the perimeter. US Army commanders later stated that USN CAS was a critical factor in saving the 8th Army from extinction. On August 1 *Philippine Sea* joined with *Valley Forge*; alternating between targets on both coasts of Korea, the carriers were active for the remainder of the month conducting interdiction and CAS missions.

Boxer, with an air group of four Corsair squadrons and one Skyraider squadron, joined the fight on the day of the landings at Inchon on September 15. The risky landing was fully successful and forced the North Koreans into headlong retreat. TF 77 then headed back to the east coast to prepare for another landing at Wonsan and was joined by *Leyte* from the Mediterranean. This marked the first time that four Essex-class carriers had operated together since World War II. The landing at Wonsan was delayed by North Korean

D ***PHILIPPINE SEA* GOES TO WAR**

One of the first USN carriers to respond to North Korean aggression in June 1950 was *Philippine Sea*. Commissioned in 1946, the ship was an unmodernized Essex-class carrier. In this view, the ship is launching strikes in August 1950 after entering combat operations. Most of the strike is already in the air, but several AD4 Skyraiders have yet to launch and are located on or near the bow catapults. Two F9F-2 Panther fighters can be seen flying over the ship. *Philippine Sea* was a "long hull" Essex-class carrier with the prominent bow to allow two 40mm quad mounts to be placed on the bow. The ship carries a full battery of 12 5in./38 guns and a heavy battery of 40mm and 20mm guns. The island features the modified bridge, the SX fighter-control radar on the mast platform, the large SK-2 antenna on the stack, and two Mark 37 directors with Mark 25 radars for the 5in. battery.

Korean War deployments by Essex-class carriers	
Antietam	1
Bon Homme Richard	2
Boxer	4
Essex	2
Kearsarge	1
Lake Champlain	1
Leyte	1
Oriskany	1
Philippine Sea	3
Princeton	3
Valley Forge	4

sea mines and did not occur until the port had already been taken by friendly ground troops. With the war looking like a quick Allied victory, all four carriers ended combat operations and returned to Japan. *Boxer* proceeded to the US for a long-overdue overhaul.

The victory parade up to the Yalu River, marking the border between North Korea and China, was ended abruptly by Chinese intervention. On November 5, TF 77 departed Japan to conduct CAS and to drop the bridges across the Yalu. This later task was made difficult by the distance from launch areas in the Sea of Japan to the target and the fact that the Panther was outclassed by the latest Chinese Communist fighter, the MiG-15. Nearly 600 sorties were flown against the Yalu bridges between November 9–21. A typical strike consisted of eight Skyraiders and 16 Corsairs carrying bombs and rockets escorted by 8–16 Panthers. The bridge-busting effort ended in failure and in any event was mounted too late to make a difference. *Valley Forge* departed for an overhaul on November 19, but the worsening situation on the ground against the Chinese intervention force of over 250,000 men forced the carrier to return after embarking *Boxer*'s air group. *Princeton* arrived in the region on December 5. The intensive efforts of TF 77, supported by two USN escort carriers and a British light carrier, contributed to the stopping of the Chinese attack by the end of 1950 and covered the retreat of an entire corps to Wonsan for embarkation. Between December 1 and 11, TF 77 flew 860 CAS sorties.

In 1951 *Leyte* returned to the US leaving *Philippine Sea*, *Princeton*, and *Valley Forge* to maintain a rotation keeping two carriers on the line with a third on a ten-day rest and replenishment period in Japan. The two carriers in the Sea of Japan conducted a replenishment at sea every fourth day and the one in Japan was on a 12-hour recall. In March, *Boxer* returned after an overhaul and relieved *Valley Forge*. The following month, TF 77 was ordered off the Chinese coast following intelligence that a Chinese invasion of Taiwan was imminent. In May *Bon Homme Richard* replaced *Philippine Sea*.

From the winter of 1950 until the middle of 1952, TF 77 shifted its focus from battlefield support to interdiction. Except for emergencies, TF 77 stopped doing CAS until the last six months of the war. The interdiction campaign began on January 29 1951 with the carriers responsible for the

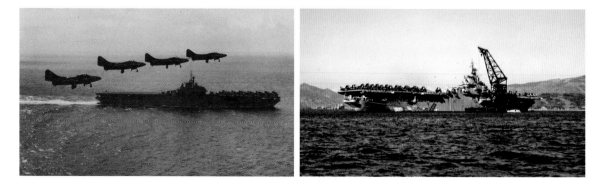

eastern half of Korea. Interdiction operations intensified in June; named Operation *Strangle*, the campaign continued until September 20. Although hundreds of trucks were claimed as destroyed and every road and bridge were subjected to 24-hour attack, American interdiction efforts were ultimately unsuccessful. In October 1951, interdiction operations shifted to rail traffic and facilities and remained a focus for the remainder of the war. By the time Operation *Strangle* ended, TF 77 included *Essex*, *Bon Homme Richard*, and *Antietam*, which had relieved *Boxer*. *Bon Homme Richard* was subsequently relieved by *Valley Forge*. *Essex* had arrived in the Sea of Japan on August 22 1951 with the first squadron of F2H Banshee aircraft and was the first modernized Essex-class carrier to see combat. Whereas losses to communist antiaircraft fire were light for the first part of the war, the threat to TF 77 aircraft increased during 1951 as more antiaircraft weapons were deployed and the use of radar for fire control increased. Between May and December 1951, TF 77 lost 74 aircraft to enemy fire.

As truce talks dragged on during mid-1952 without progress, the focus of TF 77 strike operations shifted again to specific military and infrastructure targets with the potential to cause the most pain to the Communists. Key targets included power plants, bridges, and oil refineries. In May 1951, TF 77 used World War II Mk 13 torpedoes to destroy the Hwachon Dam. USN jets were employed for the first time to escort Air Force B-29 heavy bombers against a key infrastructure target at Rashin on August 25 1951. On June 23–24, four TF 77 carriers struck the Suiho hydroelectric facility. The following month, TF 77 hit targets in and around Pyongyang. The largest single carrier strike of the war was conducted by 142 aircraft from *Boxer*, *Essex*, and *Princeton* on September 1 1952. The Aoji oil refinery was knocked out for the rest of the war, according to post-attack analysis. The infrastructure attacks were complemented by so-called Cherokee Strikes (named after TF 77's commander, "Jocko" Clark and his American Indian ancestry). Clark calculated that he could identify and cripple military targets behind the Communist front line that were beyond the range of normal CAS. These attacks were focused on military supplies. The first Cherokee attack took place on October 9 1952 and by the middle of the month 50 percent of TF 77 sorties were employed in this manner. The attacks were judged to be successful and were a valuable method of curtailing the ability of the Communists to launch a major offensive.

As the war wound down, *Oriskany* arrived in late October 1952 carrying the latest variant of the Panther, the F9F-5. *Boxer* returned in May 1953 and was later joined by *Lake Champlain*. In March 1953,

Ticonderoga spent almost all of the Cold War as an attack carrier. After being the first carrier to complete five Vietnam tours, *Ticonderoga* was the last Essex-class carrier to receive a CVS designation in 1969. This view from November 1968 shows the air group with A4 Skyhawks, F8 Crusaders, and a twin-engine A3 Skywarrior on the angle. The ship's principal radars are the large SPS-43 air search radar and the SPS-30 height finder. (Naval History and Heritage Command)

Princeton returned to TF 77, which planned to use the ship as a dedicated night carrier. This did not occur before a truce brought the war to an end on July 27 1953. The Korean War underlined the continuing importance of carrier aviation and ensured that it retained its place at the center of the Cold War USN. The versatility and utility of carrier aviation had been proven beyond a doubt. TF 77 had contributed a significant proportion of American sorties during the war. In 1950, TF 77 flew almost 3,300 sorties per month; this rose to over 4,000 sorties the following year. By the end of February 1953, nearly 4,500 sorties were being flown each month. By the end of the war, the number of missions flown by jets and propellor aircraft were equal.

Essex-class carriers and the Vietnam conflict

By the time the US actively intervened in the Vietnam War, the Essex class had been superseded by the USN's much larger "supercarriers." This secondary position did not mean that the Essex class did not play an important role in air operations over South and North Vietnam. Direct American involvement was precipitated by the Tonkin Gulf Incident off North Vietnam on August 2 1964 when a USN destroyer was attacked by North Vietnamese torpedo boats. *Ticonderoga* was operating in the South China Sea and responded by vectoring a flight of four Crusader fighters to strike the retreating North Vietnamese boats. Using their 20mm guns and rockets, they claimed one of the four boats. Two nights later, two USN destroyers reported another attack from North Vietnamese torpedo boats. The Americans saw these attacks as unprovoked attacks in international waters that demanded retaliation. On August 4, aircraft from *Ticonderoga* and *Constellation* stuck four targets in North Vietnam focusing on naval targets. Another supercarrier, *Ranger*, was sent into the region, and *Kearsarge* (an ASW carrier) was also deployed to provide protection against possible Chinese submarine attack.

The impressive USN presence in the South China Sea did not deter North Vietnam from further attacks on US personnel in South Vietnam. The next attack occurred on February 7. That same day, *Hancock* joined *Coral Sea* and *Ranger* in retaliatory strikes on targets in North Vietnam. Another North Vietnamese attack on American personnel brought another retaliatory strike

E **ANTIETAM IN 1953**

Antietam was the first USN carrier, and the first carrier in the world, to receive an angled deck. As can be seen from the overhead view, this simple idea made recovery operations possible with high-speed jets since aircraft that failed to catch an arresting wire could take off and come around again. Aside from the addition of the angled deck, *Antietam* was a "long hull" Essex-class carrier with few modifications from the original World War II configuration of those ships. All the original 5in./38 mounts are present except the two on the port-side aft sponson. The 40mm battery has been reduced by the removal of the mount forward of the bridge and on the port-side aft sponson, and the 20mm guns have been removed. The island features a post-World War II modified bridge, the SPS-6 air-search radar on the mast platform, the large SK-2 antenna on the stack, and two Mark 37 directors with Mark 25 radars for the 5in. battery.

Vietnam War deployments by Essex-class carriers	
Bennington	3 (as a CVS)
Bon Homme Richard	6
Hancock	7
Hornet	3 (as a CVS)
Intrepid	3
Kearsarge	4 (as a CVS)
Oriskany	7
Princeton	4 (as an LPH)
Shangri-La	1
Ticonderoga	5
Valley Forge	4 (as an LPH)
Yorktown	3 (as a CVS)

on February 11. These attacks were hampered by monsoon weather and heavy antiaircraft fire and were generally ineffective.

USN carriers operated from two launch areas during the Vietnam War. Yankee Station was south of Hainan Island and was utilized to strike targets primarily in North Vietnam. Beginning in May 1965, carriers operated from Dixie Station in the South China Sea to service targets in South Vietnam. Carriers arriving in the theater would usually start operations on Dixie Station and then move north after gaining combat experience to conduct operations against targets in North Vietnam, which were much better defended. Against well-defended targets, air groups executed so-called Alpha Strikes employing all available aircraft. Essex-class ships flew attack sorties with A4 Skyhawk and A1 Skyraiders. Fighter cover was provided by F8 Crusaders.

The North Vietnamese were not impressed by American retaliatory strikes, so the Americans decided to up the ante and begin a much larger air campaign called *Rolling Thunder*. The goal was nothing less than to make North Vietnam agree to peace negotiations. For a number of reasons, most of which concerned restrictions placed on operational commanders, the campaign never had a chance of success. The first part of the campaign unfolded in March 1965 with *Hancock* contributing to the effort. During the year *Bon Homme Richard* and *Oriskany* also participated in *Rolling Thunder*. The three carriers on Yankee Station in December 1965, including *Ticonderoga*, ended the year with a massive 100-aircraft attack on a large thermal power plant. Despite the efforts of ten carriers since August 1964, *Rolling Thunder* was a total failure.

Following a halt in late 1965, bombing operations resumed over North Vietnam in January 1966. The monsoon weather, stretching from November through April, hampered operations and the North Vietnamese used the bombing halt to bolster their defenses. Antiaircraft defenses over key targets were extremely heavy and included Soviet-provided SA-2 Guideline surface-to-air missiles, and modern MiG-17 and MiG-21 fighters. American losses climbed and attrition affected operations. USN

F

ORISKANY ON FIRE

On October 26 1966 *Oriskany* was struck by a major disaster. During a second Vietnam deployment, a major fire erupted onboard. The conflagration was caused by a mishandled flare – a sailor had thrown an accidentally activated Mark 24 magnesium flare into a flare locker located adjacent to the starboard sponson off the forward hangar deck. Soon the hundreds of flares in the locker ignited and burned fiercely. The fire spread into the forward hangar bay where fueled and armed aircraft were located. Some of this ordnance detonated and spread fire and smoke over four levels of the ship. Many officers were caught by smoke and fire in their nearby staterooms and died. Firefighting teams tried to cool the steel flight deck while other personnel pushed ordnance off the flight deck. In the hangar bay, aircraft engulfed in the flames were also pushed over the side together with ordnance staged in the hangar deck. At approximately 1030hrs the fire in the hangar deck was brought under control. Forty-three men died in the flames followed by one more days later. *Oriskany* was forced to return to the Philippines for immediate repairs and returned to the US for more extensive repairs.

Hornet photographed conducting a replenishment at sea with oiler *Cimarron* and destroyer *Nicholas* on Yankee Station in 1966. *Hornet* was one of four CVSs that deployed to Vietnam to provide ASW protection to TF 77 and perform plane guard duties for the attack carriers. (Naval History and Heritage Command)

BELOW RIGHT

Intrepid was the only Essex-class carrier to be designated as a CVS but subsequently used in an attack role. This view of *Intrepid* underway in the South China Sea on November 15 1968 shows part of the carrier's air group with 17 A4 Skyhawk, four F8 Crusaders, and a single A1 Skyraider arrayed on the angled deck. The ship's electronic suite has been modified with the addition of an SPS-37 air search radar and the SPS-30 height-finder radar with its dish antenna. (Naval History and Heritage Command)

FAR RIGHT

Bon Homme Richard, pictured here in the Gulf of Tonkin on April 5 1969, was the only Essex-class carrier to launch strike missions in three wars. This view shows the Vietnam-era air group with F8 Crusader fighters, A4 light strike aircraft, one E1 Tracer early warning aircraft, and an A3 Skywarrior. The Skywarrior was the heaviest aircraft to operate from Essex-class carriers; by 1969 it was used in an air refueling and electronic jamming role. (Naval History and Heritage Command)

carriers were assigned targets along the North Vietnamese coast including the key port of Haiphong.

Hancock assisted three larger carriers early in 1965. *Intrepid*, previously designated as an ASW carrier, arrived on Dixie Station in May with an air group that made the ship capable of strike operations. All *Intrepid's* ASW aircraft were sent ashore and 28 Skyhawks and 24 Skyraiders embarked. These aircraft provided outstanding ground support to Allied troops in South Vietnam flying 5,000 sorties over two months. In September and October *Intrepid* moved north to Yankee Station and added Crusaders to the ship's air group.

On October 26 1966 the largest disaster to befall any Essex-class carrier during the Vietnam War was recorded on *Oriskany*. Mishandled flares started a fire on the hangar deck that spread and ignited other ordnance. Forty-four men died and the ship was forced to return to the US for major repairs.

In early 1967 Crusaders from *Bon Homme Richard* gained multiple kills of North Vietnamese MiGs. Skyhawks from *Bon Homme Richard* debuted the Walleye TV-guided bomb in March. *Oriskany* was joined by *Intrepid* before the monsoon weather closed operations in 1967. Eleven carriers were active during the year, but despite the impressive amounts of bombs unloaded over North Vietnam, the Communists were not forced to the negotiation table.

Oriskany began 1968 alongside two larger carriers striking targets in North Vietnam. The most important event of the year was the Tet Offensive launched by Communist forces on January 30. The attack was a military failure but a political shock to the US. President Johnson imposed a partial bombing halt of North Vietnam on March 31, followed by a complete halt on November 1. During 1968, *Bon Homme Richard* and *Intrepid* participated in strike operations.

With the bombing halt still in effect during 1969, operations focused on the ground support operation over South Vietnam. Early in the year,

Hancock was one of the four carriers on station. The ship departed in February and was replaced by *Ticonderoga* with the first A7 Corsair II light attack aircraft. These replaced the much admired Skyraiders, which flew their final missions the previous year. In 1970 *Bon Homme Richard* ended a sixth and final deployment in November. *Oriskany* made a fifth deployment during the year with two A7 squadrons as part of the ship's air group. *Hancock* supported the South Vietnamese attack into Laos in 1971 with an air group still flying A4s.

When a major Communist offensive kicked off on March 30 1972, two carriers were on station, including *Hancock*. The attack was halted by American air power; by July six carriers were present, which was the largest number during the war. Among the new additions was *Oriskany*. American airpower was unleashed over North Vietnam in December 1972 and forced the North Vietnamese to return to the negotiation table. A ceasefire in January 1973 brought the war to a close. It had demonstrated the limitations of air power but confirmed the continuing utility of USN carrier aviation. It was also the last war for the Essex-class carriers. When South Vietnam fell in 1975, *Hancock* returned to assist in the evacuation of Saigon.

ESSEX-CLASS COLD WAR CAREERS

Essex

Service Dates	Conversions	Classifications	Fate
Commissioned: Dec 31 1942	SCB 27A (Feb 1949–Jan 1951)	CV 9 (as commissioned)	Scrapped 1975
Decommissioned: Jan 9 1947	SCB 125 (Aug 1955–Jan 1956)	CVA 9 (Oct 1 1952)	
Recommissioned: Jan 15 1951	Received FRAM II work in FY 62	CVS 9 (Mar 8 1960)	
Decommissioned: Jun 30 1969			

This is *Essex* underway during a Mediterranean deployment on June 22 1967. By this point the ship had received the SCB 27A and SCB 27C modernizations and had been redesignated as a CVS. CVS status is indicated by the numerous SF2 Tracker ASW aircraft on deck and the bow anchor that indicates the ship had been fitted with the SQS-23 sonar. (Naval History and Heritage Command)

After undergoing initial modernization and being recommissioned in 1951, *Essex* made two combat deployments during the Korean War. Subsequently the ship made three more Western Pacific deployments before transferring to the Atlantic Fleet in 1957. *Essex* made eight deployments to the Mediterranean and North Atlantic between 1959 and 1968, all but one as an ASW carrier. In April 1961, the carrier prepared to provide air support to the Bay of Pigs landing in Cuba with a squadron of 12 unmarked A4D Skyhawks. At the last moment, President Kennedy decided not to commit American aircraft to the operation. In October 1962, *Essex* took part in the naval quarantine of Cuba. *Essex* served as the primary recovery ship for the Apollo 7 space mission in October 1968.

Yorktown

Service Dates	Conversions	Classifications	Fate
Commissioned: Apr 15 1943	SCB 27A (Feb 15 1951–2 Jan 1953)	CV 10 (as commissioned)	Preserved as a museum ship in Charleston, South Carolina
Decommissioned: Jan 9 1947	SCB 125 (Jul 31 1954–15 Oct 1955)	CVA 10 (Oct 1 1952)	
Recommissioned: Jan 2 1953	Received FRAM II work in FY 66	CVS 10 (Jan 9 1957)	
Decommissioned: Jun 27 1970			

After an intense World War II career, *Yorktown*'s Cold War career was relatively uneventful. Brought back into active service by the Korean War, *Yorktown* made four Western Pacific deployments from 1953 to 1957 as an attack carrier. Following conversion into an ASW carrier, the ship made another four Western Pacific deployments between 1958 and 1965. Still in the ASW role, *Yorktown* made three combat tours off Vietnam between 1965 and 1968. Before being transferred to the Atlantic Fleet in 1969, the carrier was used as the primary recovery ship for the Apollo 8 mission and played a starring role in the movie *Tora!, Tora!, Tora!*, that depicted the Japanese attack on Pearl Harbor.

Intrepid

Service Dates	Conversions	Classifications	Fate
Commissioned: Aug 16 1943	SCB 27C (Sep 24 1951–Jun 18 1954)	CV 11 (as commissioned)	Preserved as a museum ship in New York City
Decommissioned: Mar 22 1947	SCB 125 (Jan 24 1956–May 2 1957)	CVA 11 (Oct 1 1952)	
Recommissioned: Jun 18 1954	Received FRAM II work 1965	CVS 11 (Mar 31 1962)	
Decommissioned: Mar 30 1974			

After an eventful combat career in World War II, *Intrepid* remained in the Far East after the war to support occupation operations before joining the reserve fleet in 1947. Recalled to duty, the carrier underwent modernization and was recommissioned in 1954. Except for three combat tours to Vietnam, *Intrepid* spent the next 20 years assigned to the Atlantic

Fleet. Before assuming the role as an ASW carrier, *Intrepid* conducted seven deployments to the Atlantic or Mediterranean. The redesignation to CVS came in 1962; following this, *Intrepid* was active in the Caribbean and Mediterranean in a new role. To spread the burden of Vietnam deployments among as many carriers as possible, the USN designated *Intrepid* as a "special attack" carrier with an attack air group while the ship maintained CVS designation. Under this arrangement, *Intrepid* conducted three combat deployments to Vietnam between 1966 and 1969. Returning to an ASW role, the carrier made three more Atlantic and Mediterranean deployments before being decommissioned in 1974. *Intrepid* was also the primary recovery ship for two space missions and is the best-known Essex-class ship by virtue of having been a museum ship in New York City since 1982.

Hornet

Service Dates	Conversions	Classifications	Fate
Commissioned: Nov 29 1943	SCB 27A (Jun 14 1951–1 Oct 1953)	CV 12 (as commissioned)	Preserved as a museum ship in Alameda, California
Decommissioned: Jan 15 1947	SCB 125 (Aug 24 1955–15 Aug 1956)	CVA 12 (Oct 1 1952)	
Recommissioned: Mar 20 1951	Received FRAM II work in FY 65	CVS 12 (Jun 27 1958)	
Decommissioned: Jun 26 1970			

Hornet is another famous World War II carrier with an uneventful Cold War career. The carrier participated in Operation *Magic Carpet* before being decommissioned for the first time in 1947. With modernization complete in 1953, *Hornet* conducted an around-the-world cruise to transfer to the Pacific Fleet. During this deployment *Hornet*'s air group was involved in the "Hainan Incident" in July 1954, when two Chinese Communist fighters were shot down in the South China Sea after they attacked US aircraft conducting searches for a missing British airliner. As a conventional carrier, *Hornet* made another three deployments to the Western Pacific between 1955 and 1958. Following redesignation as an ASW carrier, *Hornet* conducted four more Western Pacific deployments between 1959 and 1964. *Hornet* participated in the Vietnam War as an ASW carrier making three combat tours between 1966 and 1969. Aside from this World War II service, *Hornet* is probably best known as the primary recovery ships for the Apollo 11 and Apollo 12 space missions, both of which occurred in 1969.

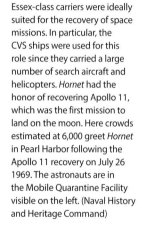

Essex-class carriers were ideally suited for the recovery of space missions. In particular, the CVS ships were used for this role since they carried a large number of search aircraft and helicopters. *Hornet* had the honor of recovering Apollo 11, which was the first mission to land on the moon. Here crowds estimated at 6,000 greet *Hornet* in Pearl Harbor following the Apollo 11 recovery on July 26 1969. The astronauts are in the Mobile Quarantine Facility visible on the left. (Naval History and Heritage Command)

Franklin

Service Dates	Conversions	Classifications	Fate
Commissioned: Jan 31 1944	None	CV 13 (as commissioned)	Scrapped 1966
Decommissioned: Feb 17 1947		CVA 13 (Oct 1 1952)	
		CVS 9 (Aug 8 1953)	
		AVT 8 (May 15 1959)	

Franklin was heavily damaged off Japan on March 19 1945; over 800 men were killed and almost 500 wounded. The ship survived despite being the most heavily damaged Essex-class carrier of the war. Fully repaired, *Franklin* was decommissioned in 1947 and was never modernized or returned to service.

Ticonderoga

Service Dates	Conversions	Classifications	Fate
Commissioned: Sep 10 1944	SCB 27C (Jul 17 1951–1 Oct 1954)	CV 14 (as commissioned)	Scrapped 1974
Decommissioned: Jan 9 1947	SCB 125 (Nov 7 1955–1 Apr 1957)	CVA 14 (Oct 1 1952)	
Recommissioned: Oct 1 1954		CVS 14 (Oct 21 1969)	
Decommissioned: Sep 1 1973			

Ticonderoga underwent modernization and was recommissioned in 1954. After one deployment to the Mediterranean in 1955–56, *Ticonderoga* spent

G **INTREPID IN 1974**

Intrepid was one of the most active World War II Essex-class carriers and one of only four still in existence. *Intrepid* was also one of the most modernized ships in the class receiving the SCB 27C, SCB 125, and the FRAM II packages. These views depict the ship in final configuration in 1974 before decommissioning. The carrier has the reworked island, angled deck, and hurricane bow. Two deck-edge elevators can be seen. Armament has been reduced to four 5in./38 single mounts. *Intrepid's* electronics suite was upgraded during the ship's FRAM II refit in 1966 and included the SPS-29 air search radar, an SPS-30 height-finder radar, and an SPS-10 surface search radar. Air traffic control was accomplished with the SPN-6, SPN-12, and SPN-35 radars; the latter was enclosed in a large radome located on the aft edge of the island. *Intrepid* remains afloat today as a museum ship in New York City.

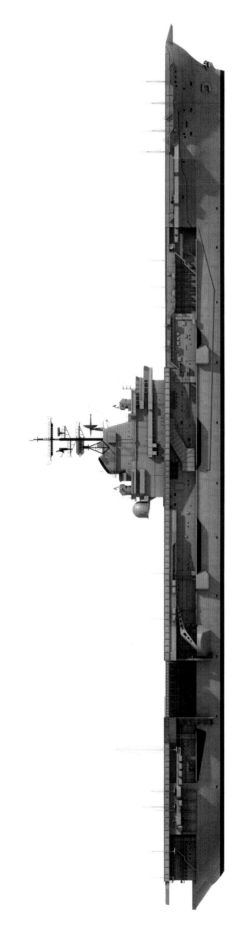
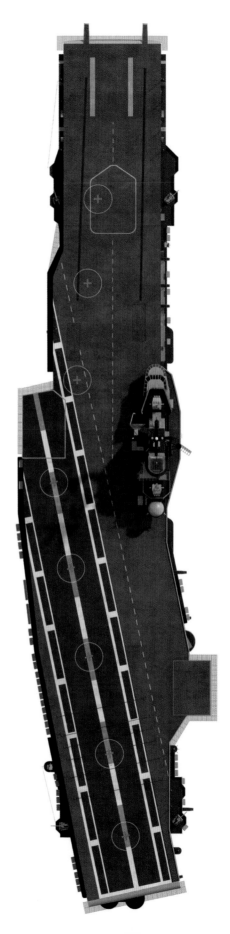

the rest of operations in the Pacific before being retired in 1973. Once assigned to the Pacific Fleet, the carrier was a regular presence in the Western Pacific making ten deployments between 1957 and 1969. The last five were combat tours to Vietnam, which made *Ticonderoga* the first carrier to complete five combat deployments. After a final Vietnam deployment, *Ticonderoga* was redesignated as a CVS in 1969 and conducted two final Western Pacific deployments in this capacity. The carrier was also the primary recovery ship for Apollo 16 and 17 in 1972.

Randolph

Service Dates	Conversions	Classifications	Fate
Commissioned: Oct 9 1944	SCB 27A (Jun 22 1951– Jul 1 1953)	CV 15 (as commissioned)	Scrapped 1975
Decommissioned: Feb 25 1948	SCB 125 (Mar 1 1955– Feb 12 1956)	CVA 15 (Oct 1 1952) CVS 15 (Mar 31 1959)	
Recommissioned: Jul 1 1953	Received FRAM II work in FY 61		
Decommissioned: Feb 13 1969			

After being recommissioned in 1953, *Randolph* spent an entire career in the Atlantic Fleet, first as an attack carrier and then as an ASW carrier. As an attack carrier, *Randolph* conducted five deployments to the Mediterranean between 1954 and 1959. Once designated as an ASW carrier, *Randolph* continued a pattern of regular Atlantic or Mediterranean deployments. Between 1962 and 1966, the carrier made nine deployments to those areas. During the first of these, the ship participated in the naval quarantine of Cuba. While prosecuting a Soviet Foxtrot-class diesel submarine on October 27, *Randolph* unwittingly almost became the target of a nuclear-armed torpedo. *Randolph* was also the primary recovery ship for two space missions, including John Glenn's first orbital flight.

Randolph photographed on February 27 1962 after being designated as a CVS. Note the two S2F Trackers on catapults. The size of these aircraft required a carrier as large as an Essex-class ship to operate them. (Naval History and Heritage Command)

Lexington

Service Dates	Conversions	Classifications	Fate
Commissioned: Mar 17 1943	SCB 27C and SCB 125 (Jul 21 1952–Sep 1 1955)	CV 16 (as commissioned)	Preserved as a museum ship in Corpus Christi, Texas
Decommissioned: Apr 23 1947		CVA 16 (Oct 1 1952)	
Recommissioned: Sep 1 1955		CVS 16 (Oct 1 1962)	
Decommissioned: Nov 8 1991		CVT 16 (Jan 1 1969)	
		AVT 16 (Jul 1 1978)	

After a full modernization concluding in 1955, *Lexington* was recommissioned and assigned to the Pacific Fleet. As an attack carrier, *Lexington* made seven Western Pacific deployments. The last deployment saw a transfer to the Atlantic Fleet. *Lexington* participated in the Cuban Missile Crisis enforcing the naval quarantine of Cuba. In January 1962, the ship was sent to the Gulf of Mexico to relieve *Antietam* as the USN's dedicated training carrier. *Lexington* was retained in this capacity for the next 22 years until decommissioning in 1991. Since the next-to-last Essex-class carrier (*Oriskany*) left active service in 1976, this made *Lexington* the longest-serving ship of the class by a wide margin.

Bunker Hill

Service Dates	Conversions	Classifications	Fate
Commissioned: May 24 1943	None	CV 17 (as commissioned)	Scrapped 1973
Decommissioned: Jan 9 1947		CVA 17 (Oct 1 1952)	
		CVS 17 (Aug 8 1953)	
		AVT 9 (May 15 1959)	

Bunker Hill was heavily damaged off Japan on May 11 1945. The attack resulted in the death of almost 400 men and injury to another 264. After completing repairs, the ship was assigned to Operation *Magic Carpet* before being decommissioned in 1947. *Bunker Hill* and *Franklin* were the only two Essex-class carriers never to be modernized or returned to service.

Wasp

Service Dates	Conversions	Classifications	Fate
Commissioned: Nov 24 1943	SCB 27A (Sep 1 1948–Sep 28 1951)	CV 18 (as commissioned)	Scrapped 1973
Decommissioned: Feb 17 1947	SCB 125 (Jul 31 1954–Dec 1 1955)	CVA 18 (Oct 1 1952)	
Recommissioned: Sep 28 1951	Received FRAM II work in FY 65	CVS 18 (Nov 1 1956)	
Decommissioned: Jul 1 1972			

Immediately after World War II, *Wasp* participated in Operation *Magic Carpet*. After a short period in the reserve fleet, the ship was one of the first carriers selected for SCB 27A modernization. Following this work, en route to the Mediterranean, *Wasp* collided with destroyer minesweeper *Hobson* on April 26 1952. *Hobson* sank with the loss of 176 men. *Wasp* was forced to return to the US and, in only ten days, received a new bow from *Hornet* which was undergoing modernization in New York at the time. *Wasp* was able to resume interrupted Mediterranean deployment. In 1953–54 *Wasp* conducted an around-the-world cruise and transferred to the Pacific Fleet. As an attack carrier, *Wasp* made two deployments to the Western Pacific in 1955–1956. Following redesignation as an ASW carrier, *Wasp* returned to and remained with the Atlantic Fleet. Before decommissioning in 1972, *Wasp* conducted eight Atlantic or Mediterranean deployments. These included participating in the Lebanon crisis of 1958. In addition, the carrier supported three Gemini space events in 1965 and another in 1966. *Wasp* also had more than a fair share of accidents, including a major fire on the hangar deck in August 1959 and two collisions with oilers in 1967 and 1968.

Hancock

Service Dates	Conversions	Classifications	Fate
Commissioned: Apr 15 1944	SCB 27C (17 Jul 1951–Mar 1 1954)	CV 19 (as commissioned)	Scrapped 1976
Decommissioned: May 9 1947	SCB 125 (Aug 24 1955–Nov 15 1956)	CVA 19 (Oct 1 1952)	
Recommissioned: Mar 1 1954			
Decommissioned: Jan 30 1976			

Hancock was one of the few Essex-class carriers to receive full modernization but remain as an attack carrier. After completing modernization, the carrier made seven deployments to the Western Pacific between 1955 and 1963. *Hancock*'s wartime career began in October 1964 with a first combat deployment to the waters off Vietnam. Six more combat tours followed giving *Hancock* the most combat deployments during the war tied with *Oriskany* among Essex-class carriers. After active US involvement in the war ended, *Hancock* was still involved in the war's aftermath. As an ad hoc helicopter carrier, the ship participated in the evacuations from Phnom Penh, Cambodia and Saigon, Vietnam in 1975.

Bennington

Service Dates	Conversions	Classifications	Fate
Commissioned: Aug 6 1944	SCB 27A (1950–1952)	CV 20 (as commissioned)	Scrapped 1994
Decommissioned: Nov 8 1946	SCB 125 (Jun 1954– Mar 1955)	CVA 20 (Oct 1 1952)	
Recommissioned: Nov 13 1952	Received FRAM II work FY 63	CVS 20 (Jun 30 1959)	
Decommissioned: Jan 15 1970			

Bennington transferred to the Pacific Fleet in 1955 and thus missed the Korean War. As an ASW carrier, the ship made six deployments in the Pacific including three to Vietnam between 1965 and 1968. After being recommissioned, *Bennington* suffered two major accidents. In April 1953 a boiler exploded and killed 11 crewmen. The following year, the port catapult hydraulic accumulator burst, which resulted in the deaths of 102 men with 201 wounded.

Bennington pictured off the coast of California in November 1967. The presence of a bow anchor indicates that an SQS-23 bow sonar dome was fitted during the ship's FRAM II refit in 1963. The angled bump-out under the island is the escalator fitted to move pilots from their ready rooms to the flight deck. (Naval History and Heritage Command)

Boxer

Service Dates	Conversions	Classifications	Fate
Commissioned: Apr 16 1945	None	CV 21 (as commissioned)	Scrapped 1971
Decommissioned: Dec 1 1969		CVA 21 (Oct 1 1952)	
		CVS 21 (Feb 1 1956)	
		LPH 4 (Jan 30 1959)	

Commissioned too late to see action in World War II, *Boxer* conducted two peacetime Pacific deployments before the start of the Korean War. After the outbreak of war in Korea, in July 1950 the carrier was used as a high-speed aircraft transport for 145 P-51 Mustang fighters (as well as assorted other aircraft, over 1,000 Air Force personnel, and other supplies) and arrived in Japan after a record-breaking eight-day transit of the Pacific (the return transit broke the record again in just under seven and a half days). *Boxer* became the third Essex-class carrier to enter combat when the ship returned to Korea in September 1950 for the first of four combat deployments (most of the war, tied with *Valley Forge*). During the third deployment, on 5 August 1952, fire broke out on the hangar deck and spread among the aircraft being readied for the next day's strike. Despite the conflagration, only seven men were killed, but 12 aircraft were destroyed. After the Korean War, *Boxer* did not receive any modernization. After conducting two more Pacific deployments between 1954 and 1956 as an attack carrier, the ship was redesignated as an ASW carrier in 1956 and conducted two more Pacific deployments in this role. *Boxer* began a new career as an LPH in 1959 and was assigned to the Atlantic Fleet. As an LPH *Boxer* was active during the Cuban Missile Crisis in 1962, made a Mediterranean deployment in 1964, participated in the occupation of the Dominican Republic in 1965, and made two helicopter ferry runs to Vietnam. *Boxer* was also the primary recovery ship for two space events. When decommissioned in 1969 after 25 years of continuous service, *Boxer* still maintained the basic configuration of a World War II-era Essex-class carrier.

Bon Homme Richard

Service Dates	Conversions	Classifications	Fate
Commissioned: Nov 26 1944	SCB 27C and SCB 125 (May 1953–Nov 1955)	CV 31 (as commissioned)	Scrapped 1992
Decommissioned: Jan 9 1947		CVA 31 (Oct 1 1952)	
Recommissioned: Jan 15 1951			
Decommissioned: Jul 2 1971			

Bon Homme Richard was the only Essex-class ship to participate in three wars in a conventional carrier role. The ship arrived in the Pacific in time to join the Third Fleet in the final raids on Japan from June to August 1945. After the end of hostilities, the carrier was converted into a temporary troop transport to take part in Operation *Magic Carpet*. *Bon Homme Richard* was briefly out of commission from 1947 to 1951 until the Korean War brought the carrier out of reserve. In an unmodernized state, *Bon Homme Richard* conducted two combat deployments to Korea. The ship underwent extensive modernization from 1953 to '55 receiving the SCB 27C and SCB 125 upgrades in one yard period, and was one of only three Essex-class ships to get both packages together. After modernization, *Bon Homme Richard* was assigned to the Pacific Fleet and remained there. From 1956 to 1963, the ship conducted six Western Pacific deployments and began a third war in 1964 when US forces actively intervened in Vietnam. This was followed by another five combat deployments to Vietnam up until 1970. Shortly after final deployment and after some 22 years of active service, *Bon Homme Richard* was decommissioned for the last time in 1971.

Leyte

Service Dates	Conversions	Classifications	Fate
Commissioned: Apr 11 1946	None	CV 32 (as commissioned)	Scrapped 1970
Decommissioned: May 15 1959		CVA 32 (Oct 1 1952)	
		CVS 32 (Aug 8 1953)	
		AVT 10 (May 15 1959)	

Following commissioning in 1946, *Leyte* remained in the Atlantic Fleet and conducted three Mediterranean deployments between 1947 and 1950. *Leyte* was dispatched to the Pacific in late 1950 and joined combat operations in Korea on October 9. In only 92 days of combat, *Leyte*'s air group flew 3,933 combat sorties. After this combat deployment, *Leyte* returned to the Atlantic Fleet and resumed regular Mediterranean deployments in 1951 and 1952. While under conversion to a new role as a CVS, the ship suffered an explosion in the port catapult machinery room on October 16 1953 that killed 37 men and wounded another 28. *Leyte* remained active for another six years as a CVS but did not conduct any deployments before being retired in 1959.

Leyte conducted one combat deployment to Korea from October 1950 to January 1951. This is the ship moored in Yokosuka, Japan, during a replenishment period on December 1 1950. The ship is little changed from the appearance of a World War II Essex-class carrier and even carries some 20mm mounts. Aside from some changes in the electronics suite and the removal of some of the light antiaircraft guns, *Leyte* was in this configuration when retired in 1959. (Naval History and Heritage Command)

Kearsarge

Service Dates	Conversions	Classifications	Fate
Commissioned: Mar 2 1946	SCB 27A (Jan 27 1950–Mar 1 1952)	CV 33 (as commissioned)	Scrapped 1974
Decommissioned: Jun 16 1950	SCB 125 (Jan 27 1956–Jan 31 1957)	CVA 33 (Oct 1 1952)	
Recommissioned: Mar 1 1952	Received FRAM II work Nov 1961–August 1962	CVS 33 (Oct 1 1958)	
Decommissioned: Feb 13 1970			

After entering service, *Kearsarge* conducted one deployment to the Atlantic Ocean in 1947 and one to the Mediterranean in 1948. The carrier was then transferred to the Pacific Fleet and made one combat deployment to Korean waters. Between 1953 and 1958, *Kearsarge* conducted another four deployments to the Western Pacific as an attack carrier. Once redesignated as an ASW carrier, *Kearsarge* was one of the busiest CVSs in the fleet. From 1959 to 1969, the ship made 11 deployments of various lengths as a member of the Pacific Fleet. The last four of these, from 1964 to 1969, were off the coast of Vietnam to provide ASW protection to TF 77. Two deployments were made as primary recovery ships for space events.

Oriskany

Service Dates	Conversions	Classifications	Fate
Commissioned: Sep 25 1950	SCB 27A (Aug 1947–Sep 1950)	CV 34 (as commissioned)	Sunk as artificial reef on May 17 2006
Decommissioned: Sep 30 1976	SCB 125A (Sep 8 1957–May 29 1959)	CVA 34 (Oct 1 1952)	
		CV 34 (Sep 30 1976)	

Oriskany had one of the most interesting Cold War careers of any Essex-class carrier. Aside from training carrier *Lexington*, *Oriskany* was the longest-serving Essex-class carrier. The ship was launched after World War II on October 13 1945. Construction was suspended on August 22 1946 when the ship was 85 percent complete. In a partial state of completion, *Oriskany* was selected to be the prototype for Essex-class reconstruction under the SCB 27A program. To begin the modernization, the carrier was reduced to 60 percent completion and was finally commissioned in September 1950. After completion, *Oriskany* conducted one Mediterranean deployment in 1951 before transferring to the Pacific Fleet. *Oriskany*'s first Pacific deployment was a combat tour to Korea. From 1952 to 1976, *Oriskany* made another 15 Pacific deployments. Seven of these were combat deployments to Vietnam. On the second Vietnam tour, the carrier experienced a major fire on October 26 1966 that killed 44 crewmen. These seven combat tours to Vietnam made *Oriskany* the most active Essex-class ship in the war. *Oriskany* was decommissioned in 1976 and placed in reserve. During the Reagan-era naval build-up, persistent proposals were made to return *Oriskany* to service. For many reasons, primarily because of the lack of modern aircraft able to operate from the ship's relatively small deck, this never moved beyond the proposal phase. *Oriskany* was sold for scrap in 1995 but then languished until being repossessed by the USN in 1997. After remediation to remove toxic materials, *Oriskany* was finally sunk as an artificial reef off Pensacola, Florida in 2006.

Antietam

Service Dates	Conversions	Classifications	Fate
Commissioned: Jan 28 1945	None	CV 36 (as commissioned)	Scrapped 1974
Decommissioned: Jun 21 1949	Received angled deck Sep–Dec 1952	CVA 36 (Oct 1 1952)	
Recommissioned: Jul 17 1951		CVS 36 (Aug 8 1953)	
Decommissioned: May 8 1963			

Aside from the addition of an angled deck, *Antietam* was never modernized. After briefly operating as a CVS, *Antietam* was assigned as the USN's permanent training carrier in 1957. This view shows *Antietam* operating training aircraft in April 1961. The training aircraft, painted in the USN's distinctive white and orange scheme, include T2J Buckeyes amidships and forward and AD Skyraiders aft. Note the mothballed 5in./38 guns in the port-side sponsons. (Naval History and Heritage Command)

Antietam arrived in the Pacific just as the war was ending in 1945 and remained in the region for the next three years supporting occupation operations in China and Korea. Upon returning to the US, *Antietam* was decommissioned in June 1949. This break in active service was very short; by January 1951 the carrier was back in commission and headed to Korea for one, single combat deployment. After returning to the US, *Antietam* was selected for conversion into the world's first carrier with a true angled deck. Installation of the angled deck took place between September and December 1952; subsequent trials showed this feature to be a major advance in naval aviation. After being designated as an ASW carrier, *Antietam* conducted two deployments to the Mediterranean and the Atlantic. In April 1957, *Antietam* assumed duties as a dedicated training carrier until being relieved by *Lexington* in October 1962.

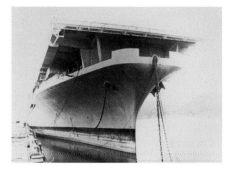 

Princeton

Service Dates	Conversions	Classifications	Fate
Commissioned: Nov 18 1945	None	CV 37 (as commissioned)	Scrapped 1971
Decommissioned: Jun 21 1949		CVA 37 (Oct 1 1952)	
Recommissioned: Aug 28 1950		CVS 37 (Jan 1 1954)	
Decommissioned: Jan 30 1970		LPH 5 (Mar 2 1959)	

Princeton was one of three Essex-class carriers to commission as an attack carrier, then serve as an ASW carrier, and end as an amphibious assault ship. Commissioned after World War II, *Princeton* was one of the newest Essex-class carriers and never received significant modernization. After three Western Pacific deployments, *Princeton* was decommissioned in 1949. After only 15 months in reserve, the carrier was reactivated for the Korean War. *Princeton* joined TF 77 in December 1950 and made a total of three combat deployments during the Korean War. Shortly after the Korean War *Princeton* was redesignated as an ASW carrier and served in this capacity for the next five years as part of the Pacific Fleet. In 1959 *Princeton* underwent conversion into an amphibious assault ship, but maintained World War II configuration until the end. As an LPH, *Princeton* made four combat deployments to the waters off Vietnam between 1965 and 1969. *Princeton* was the primary recovery ship for one space event in 1969.

Shangri-La

Service Dates	Conversions	Classifications	Fate
Commissioned: Sep 15 1944	SCB 27C and SCB 125 (Jul 17 1951–Feb 1 1955)	CV 38 (as commissioned)	Scrapped 1988
Decommissioned: Nov 7 1947		CVA 38 (Oct 1 1952)	
Recommissioned: May 10 1951		CVS 39 (Jun 30 1969)	
Decommissioned: Jul 30 1971			

Commissioned late in World War II, *Shangri-La* began combat operations in the Western Pacific in April 1945. *Shangri-La* participated in the atomic test at Bikini Atoll in the Marshall Islands (Operation *Crossroads*) in 1946 and, after a very short initial career, was placed into reserve in late 1947. Like many other Essex-class carriers, *Shangri-La* was given a new lease of life by the Korean War. After being reactivated, the carrier was selected for modernization that began in 1951. After completion, *Shangri-La* became the second USN carrier fitted with an angled deck. From 1956 to 1960, the ship conducted deployments to the Western Pacific. Still operating as an attack carrier, *Shangri-La* transferred to the Atlantic Fleet and operated in the Atlantic and Mediterranean from 1961 to 1970. Though designated an ASW carrier in 1969, *Shangri-La* never served in that role. *Shangri-La* last deployment was an arduous one lasting over nine months and included a combat deployment to the waters off Vietnam.

Lake Champlain

Service Dates	Conversions	Classifications	Fate
Commissioned: Jun 3 1945	SCB 27A (Aug 18 1950– Sep 19 1952)	CV 39 (as commissioned)	Scrapped 1972
Decommissioned: Feb 17 1947		CVA 39 (Oct 1 1952)	
Recommissioned: Sep 19 1952		CVS 39 (Aug 21 1957)	
Decommissioned: May 2 1966		AVT 12 (May 1961)	

After commissioning, *Lake Champlain* performed Operation *Magic Carpet* duties bringing troops back from Europe. After an active career of less than two years, the carrier was placed into reserve in 1947. The Korean War brought a new lease of life, and the ship was reactivated and modernized beginning in 1950. *Lake Champlain* was the only Essex-class carrier that received an SCB 27A modernization but never got an angled deck or hurricane bow. Once recommissioned, the carrier proceeded to the waters off Korea and conducted strikes for the last month of the Korean War. *Lake Champlain* spent the rest of operations assigned to the Atlantic Fleet conducting several Mediterranean

Lake Champlain anchored at Cannes, France, on June 17 1957, during final deployment as an attack aircraft carrier. This view shows an Essex-class ship after an SCB 27A modernization. A full battery of eight 5in./38 guns is fitted and all 3in./50 positions are equipped with twin mounts except the bow positions. Radars include the SPS-8A height finder in front of the pole mast and SPS-6 and SC-5 air search radars. Note that the air group includes three AJ Savage attack aircraft for atomic strike missions. (Naval History and Heritage Command)

Tarawa underway in the Mediterranean Sea in December 1952. The ship retains the configuration of a World War II Essex-class carrier, even down to retaining 40mm quad mounts. The only nod to modernity is the F2H Banshee jet fighters on the ship's catapults. (Naval History and Heritage Command)

deployments, once as a conventional carrier and then as an ASW carrier. *Lake Champlain* participated in the naval quarantine of Cuba in 1962 and was the lead recovery ship for three space events from 1961 to 1966.

Tarawa

Service Dates	Conversions	Classifications	Fate
Commissioned: Dec 8 1945	None	CV 40 (as commissioned)	Scrapped 1968
Decommissioned: Jun 30 1949		CVA 40 (Oct 1 1952)	
Recommissioned: Feb 3 1951		CVS 40 (Jan 10 1955)	
Decommissioned: May 13 1960		AVT 12 (May 1961)	

Commissioned after World War II, and never modernized, *Tarawa* was the only Essex-class ship never to see combat. Arriving in the Western Pacific in late 1946, *Tarawa* was only active until June 1949. With the start of hostilities in Korea, the carrier quickly returned to service in early 1951. Converted to an ASW carrier in late 1954–early 1955, *Tarawa* joined the Atlantic Fleet before leaving active service in 1960.

Valley Forge

Service Dates	Conversions	Classifications	Fate
Commissioned: Nov 3 1946	None	CV 45 (as commissioned)	Scrapped 1971
Decommissioned: Jan 15 1970		CVA 45 (Oct 1 1952)	
		CVS 39 (Nov 12 1953)	
		LPH 8 (Jul 1 1961)	

Valley Forge had an unusual and busy Cold War career. Aside from *Oriskany*, this ship was the last Essex-class carrier to be commissioned. Because of this, the carrier was kept in active service after World War II and was never decommissioned and never received any major modernization; the carrier always retained a basic World War II appearance. When the Korean War broke out, *Valley Forge* was the first USN carrier to conduct sorties in support of UN forces. *Valley Forge* and *Boxer* were the only carriers to conduct four combat tours during the Korean War. After the Korean War, *Valley Forge* was redesignated as an ASW carrier and served in this capacity in the Atlantic and Caribbean. In 1961 the carrier underwent conversion into an amphibious assault ship. Since these modifications were primarily internal, *Valley Forge* retained basic World War II configuration. *Valley Forge* was one of the busiest Essex-class carriers during the Vietnam War making four deployments between 1964 and 1969 as an LPH, and was the primary recovery ship for a space event in 1960.

Philippine Sea

Service Dates	Conversions	Classifications	Fate
Commissioned: May 11 1946	None	CV 47 (as commissioned)	Scrapped 1971
Decommissioned: Dec 28 1958		CVA 47 (Oct 1 1952)	
		CVS 39 (Nov 15 1955)	
		AVT 11 (May 15 1959)	

Philippine Sea was the last Essex-class carrier completed, but was commissioned six months before *Valley Forge*. After commissioning, the ship was dispatched to Antarctica in early 1947 as part of Operation *Highjump*. The carrier embarked six large transport aircraft and two smaller aircraft, along with other supplies, for the expedition led by Rear Admiral Richard Byrd. Before transferring to the Pacific Fleet in May 1950, *Philippine Sea* conducted two deployments to the Mediterranean and one to the Atlantic. When the North Koreans invaded the south, *Philippine Sea* was ordered to proceed across the Pacific at high speed and arrived in the waters off Korea on August 1 and immediately began strike operations; the second Essex-class carrier to enter the war. In total, *Philippine Sea* made three combat deployments to Korean waters. After the Korean armistice, the carrier made another four deployments to the Western Pacific, the last two as an ASW carrier. After a short 12-year active career, *Philippine Sea* was decommissioned in 1958.

Valley Forge steaming in formation in November 1958 with six destroyers as part of ASW exercises in the Atlantic during the carrier's brief career as a CVS. *Valley Forge* received no major modernization during an entire career of over 23 years. (Naval History and Heritage Command)

CONCLUSION

After stellar service in World War II, the Essex class continued as the centerpiece of the Cold War USN through the 1950s. This was only possible because of the soundness of the Essex class's original design and its ability to take extensive modernizations. However, the quick pace of development for naval aircraft meant that the days of these stalwart carriers were numbered. As early as the Korean War, USN carrier air groups were flying inferior fighters since the Navy did not want to develop swept-wing fighters that the Essex class could not safely operate. In spite of this limitation, Essex-class air groups performed admirably by virtue of their superior air crew training and solid tactics. The carriers were able to generate about 100 sorties per day in good weather and about 85 sorties per day in bad weather.

Introduction of the angled deck gave the Essex class a new, if temporary, lease of life. It allowed swept-wing and even supersonic aircraft to operate from their decks. Going into the Vietnam War, the Essex class was still an important part of USN naval air power since the ships could still operate an air group with the dependable A1 Skyraider in the heavy-attack role, A4 Skyhawks in the light attack role, and the F8 Crusader fighters that proved the most capable USN fighter against North Vietnamese fighters (probably because the squadrons flying the Crusader focused on the air combat mission). The supercarriers in the fleet demonstrated the inadequacies of the Essex class with its smaller air group, inability to operate the latest aircraft (such as the multi-mission F4 Phantom II), and inferior fuel and ordnance storage capacities. In spite of these handicaps, the six Essex-class carriers operating as attack carriers during the war performed well, but they were clearly overshadowed by the supercarriers.

In addition to its power projection missions during the Korean and Vietnam wars, the Essex class was also an important component in the USN's plan to deal with the Soviet Navy's submarine force. Against Soviet diesel submarines, the Hunter-Killer Group concept would have been successful, but against Soviet nuclear submarines the prospects for success were much reduced. In any event, the assessment that the Soviets were prepared to fight another battle for the North Atlantic against Allied sea lines of communications was overplayed, and thankfully the Essex class was never tested in its ASW role.

It is just as well that the modernized Essex-class ships were never tested against an opponent with well-developed antisurface warfare capabilities.

BELOW LEFT
Carriers *America* (on left), *Enterprise* (center), and *Oriskany* (right) steam together in the South China Sea after the fall of South Vietnam in 1975. The smaller size of *Oriskany* is quite obvious, as is the ship's limited capabilities compared to the newer generation of supercarriers. (Naval History and Heritage Command)

BELOW RIGHT
Shangri-La photographed in August 1960. By this point, the ship's primary electronics consisted of SPS-37 and SPS-12 radars, and a SPS-8A height finder. No 3in./50 mounts remained, and the 5in. battery had been reduced. Aircraft on the forward flight deck include F8U and F4D fighters, and A4D and AD attack aircraft. (Naval History and Heritage Command)

The ships possessed marginal stability and thus a reduced ability to take damage. Fortunately, they were never exposed to underwater damage after World War II and this lack of stability never became an issue in combat. Each time more radars were added, and heavier aircraft embarked, weight compensation was required. This meant the ships were basically unarmed by the end of their careers though the weapons being removed had increasingly little value against modern air or cruise missile attack. Given their declining survivability in high-threat environments and the manpower requirements to keep them running, combined with the difficulty in maintaining these older ships, they reached the end of their useful lives by the end of the 1960s. The Essex class had dominated one war for the USN, acted as the central part of the USN's naval air campaign in another war, and still gave valuable service in a third war, over 20 years after the ships in the class first entered service. This is a record unmatched by any other class of ships in naval history.

BIBLIOGRAPHY

Bonner, Kit and Carolyn, *Cold War at Sea*, Osceola, WI: MBI Publishing Company (2000)

Budzbon, Przemyslaw, Chumbley, Stephen and Gardiner, Robert, *Conway's All the World's Fighting Ships 1947–1995*, Annapolis, MD: Naval Institute Press (1996)

Dictionary of American Naval Fighting Ships found at the Navy History and Heritage Command website

Faltum, Andrew, *The Essex Aircraft Carriers*, Charleston, SC: The Nautical & Aviation Publishing Company of America (1996)

Friedman, Norman, *Naval Radar*, London: Conway Maritime Press (1981)

Friedman, Norman, *U.S. Aircraft Carriers*, Annapolis, MD: Naval Institute Press (1983)

Hallion, Richard P., *The Naval Air War in Korea*, Baltimore, MD: The Nautical & Aviation Publishing Company of America (1986)

Jane's Fighting Ships (various editions)

Mersky, Peter B. and Polmar, Norman, *The Naval Air War in Vietnam*, Annapolis, MD: The Nautical & Aviation Publishing Company of America (1981)

Muir, Malcolm, *Black Shoes and Blue Water*, Washington: Naval Historical Center (1996)

Nichols, John B. and Tillman, Barrett, *On Yankee Station*, Annapolis, MD: Naval Institute Press (1987)

Polmar, Norman, *Chronology of the Cold War at Sea 1945–1991,* Annapolis, MD: Naval Institute Press (1988)

Polmar, Norman and O'Connell, John, *Strike from the Sea*, Annapolis, MD: Naval Institute Press (2020)

Silverstone, Paul H., *The Navy of the Nuclear Age 1947–2007*, New York: Routledge (2009)

Terzibaschitsch, Stefan, *Aircraft carriers of the US Navy*, New York: Mayflower Books (1980)

The Ships and Aircraft of the U.S. Fleet (various editions), Annapolis, MD: Naval Institute Press

Winkler, David F., *Incidents at Sea*, Annapolis, MD: Naval Institute Press (2017)

INDEX